A Universal Belonging

A Universal Belonging

Poems by

Patsy Asuncion

© 2025 Patsy Asuncion. All rights reserved.
This material may not be reproduced in any form, published,
reprinted, recorded, performed, broadcast,
rewritten, or redistributed without
the explicit permission of Patsy Asuncion.
All such actions are strictly prohibited by law.

Cover design by Shay Culligan
Author photo by Patsy Asuncion

ISBN: 978-1-63980-784-0
Library of Congress Control Number: 2025942851

Kelsay Books
502 South 1040 East, A-119
American Fork, Utah 84003
Kelsaybooks.com

Acknowledgments

Select poems have appeared in some form in other publications—

About Place Journal: "Lonely George is Dead"
The Amazine: "Fisheating Creek"
Armadillo Anthology: "Fisheating Creek"
Fredericksburg Literary Art Journal: "One"
Fredericksburg: FLAR: "A Seed for a Seed," "Water Percolates Existence"
Indiana University Journal: "The Long Breaths of Trees"
New York Times: "One"
One Page Poetry Anthology: "Whole Soil Web"
Poetry Society of Virginia: "Habits of American Habitat."
South FL Writers Association: "Lonely George is Dead"
Vox Poetica: "Extant," "Acid Brew," "Nonnative Species," "Relentless Winter"
Vox Poetica: "Up in Smoke, Fogbound"

Contents

1. Earth

Long Breaths of Trees	17
Path of Patience	18
Awakening	19
Chameleon Forests	20
Involuntary Attention	21
Bone Yard	22
Farewell Old Friends	23
Nature's Passage 1 of 2	24
Nature's Passage 2 of 2	25
Full Bloom	26
Hardihood	27
Peace	28
Above the Darkness	29
Road to *Leenan*	30
Summer in the South of France	31
Three Sisters	32
Whole Soil Web	33

2. Fire

Acid Brew	37
Black Hole	38
Road to *Hana*	39
Serenity	40
Bus Stop	41
Change of Heart	42
Habits of American Habitat	43
Paradise Lost	44
Nonnative Species 1 of 2	45
Nonnative Species 2 of 2	46

Clearcutting	47
Extant	48
Lonely George Is Dead 1 of 2	49
Lonely George Is Dead 2 of 2	50
Strip Mall Apocalypse	51
Relentless Winter	52
Chosen Moments 1 of 2	53
Chosen Moments 2 of 2	54
Unseen Seen 1 of 2	55
Unseen Seen 2 of 2	56
Recede into the Noise of Everyday Memory	57
Provocation	58
Up in Smoke	59
Yoshino Cherry Tree	60
Lunch Encounter	61
Making Way	62
A Universal of Belonging	63

3. Air

Mountainous Hush	67
A Seed for a Seed 1 of 2	68
A Seed for a Seed 2 of 2	69
Do You Hear the Birds? 1 of 2	70
Do You Hear the Birds? 2 of 2	71
Gilded Silver Face 1 of 2	72
Gilded Silver Face 2 of 2	73
Drakes	74
Nest Building	75
Fogbound	76
Pileated Pearls	77

Surviving the Unsurvivable	78
Nature's Eye	79
The Moon	80
Universal Language 1 of 2	81
Universal Language 2 of 2	82
Tropical Toll	83
One	84

4. Water

Confluence	87
Holy Place	88
Ivy Creek	89
Loxahatchee	90
Palma de Mallorca	91
Matolius River	92
Mosquito Coast	93
Orcas	94
Penny the Shrimp	95
Road from *Lisboa*	96
St. Joe Shore	97
Rainy Days	98
Riverview Park Trail	99
Fisheating Creek	100
St. Patrick's Well	101
Ten Thousand Islands 1 of 2	102
Ten Thousand Islands 2 of 2	103
Sultry Suwanee 1 of 2	104
Sultry Suwanee 2 of 2	105
Water Percolates Existence	106

We are all connected . . .
To each other, biologically . . .
To the earth, chemically . . .
To the rest of the universe
atomically.
Not only are we in the
universe,
the universe is in us.

—Neil deGrasse Tyson

1. Earth

*The earth does not
belong to us,
We belong to the earth.*

—Chief Seattle

Long Breaths of Trees

Trees are sanctuaries . . . they do not preach
learning and precepts, they preach,
undeterred by particulars, the ancient law of life.
—Herman Hesse

She stands silently   allows temperate ribbons
of air to muss her premature leaves
born this last month of winter

Mother Tree   observes surrounding ponds   pardoned early from
frigid imprisonment
black bears awakened   before the alarm buzzes

precocious teen maple trees   with adult limbs
Undeterred by particulars of centuries
massive tree roots rest   in the infinity

of life-giving force   to her blended family
oak saplings   grizzlies   pileated woodpeckers
wood mice   bark beetles   carpenter ants

The symbiotic forest tribe   bends as one
around the *season creep*   of global changes
caused by men   focused on finite turfdoms

Path of Patience

A maple sapling steadies
in friendly soil   during rush hour
Spindly branches with scant leaves
peak through   in meditative repose

Since sprouting   its whole body breathes
looks up at sun and sky
Morning runners do not notice
too busy checking clocks

A distance from the path   a cluster of
teenage oaks gather   their rhythmic breaths
entreat   a surrounding   stand of mature oak
to join their chorus

People observe the greenery as
an inanimate painting   as a backdrop
for casual exploration
not communication

The patience of these Virginia woods remains
hallmark   Homey tree roots   neighborly forest floor
outstretched treetops   offer food   water   shelter
for all life   without need for notice by passersby

Awakening

Obedient leaves
soldier on
like faceless recruits
into stark scapes
abandoned
by the sun

One in front of another
they creep
by vine and branch
infiltrate
arduous rock and tar
fight
under cover of night
for scarce rations

A few survive
the battlefield
defy darkness
bloom

Raucous colors
  savage violet
  jazzed yellow
  bawdy red
burst
the quiet sky

Chameleon Forests

Subtle shades of early Mountain Laurel
change to deeper green tapestries in high

heat   punctuated by bold gangs of lilies
Black-Eyed-Susans   Mimosa   Rhododendron

First chilled breath brings red maple   golden oak
orange birch   Year end white   invites

introspective retreat of   barren branches
and retiring waters   interrupted by evergreens

Involuntary Attention

A walk in nature, walks the soul back home.
—Mary Davis

I walk the green

  once inside   I am slowed
    to the pace of the forest
      by an internal whisper

  once inside   half-closed eyelids
    blur details   sense rolling verdigris hues
      leaves trees wildflowers grass

      one living canvas
        neighborhoods   firs oaks birch tulip
          each green distinct

  once inside   ears clear
    fine tune to one voice of
      interspecies connection

      high-pitched *chirps* of spring peppers
        tu-a-wee warbles of Eastern bluebirds
          churrs rattle screeches of woodpeckers

  once inside   steps slow   on Virginia footpath for
    gray squirrels   red foxes   black bears
      swallowtails   click beetles   wolf spiders

I walk the green

  as woodlands
    enter
      my own insides

Bone Yard

RIP Dale

*Life ends with a snap of small bones,
a head cracked from its stem, and a spirit unmoored . . .*
—Sarah Kernochan

Wilted leaves, dressed in weepy black, the first
to know your absence shifted to disrobed loss.

Winter did its best to remove hangers-on,
ardent sedge blades and pansies reseeded

stubbornly along the curb of your steps.
Resolute soldiers at a requiem, upright stalks

insisted on silent watch for your return as
ghost ground cried inconsolably.

Shaped by your sure hands to thwart uninvited deer,
garden wire seemed sunken in lost purpose.

Warm weather never bothered to clean up,
stubbled weeds left unshaven for weeks.

We'd once prided in our well-turned gardens.
I grieved the loss of your neighborly green thumb.

For a season, bereavement upheaved the landscape
of people and plants, but new buds unfurled.

Old cultivars made their way to my side and
neighbors helped put your land back on its feet.

The deer are still not welcome for dinner, but
I'll leave that for you to resolve.

Farewell Old Friends

I'm still sorting through 38 Florida years.
How can I say these words to you if
I haven't even told myself I'm leaving.
Speaking aloud makes the move real.

Forever I've cared for you all and
you've returned loyal companionship.
Some of you will journey with me to a new home.
Others might not survive the trip.

My furtive glances weigh your vulnerabilities—
curved, wilting edges of age
easily broken limbs, frail flowers.
Transplanting homes rattle comfortable habits.

Crown of thorns won't let me go without her.
Snake plant is a self-sufficient traveler.
Christmas cactus, succulents are road warriors.
Croton, spider plant travel light, only basics.

Part of my heart I leave with the rest of you—
palms and *ferns*—my first friends in the sun,
poinsettia—personal idol of style, a fashionista,
pentas and *marmalades*—wild, colorful partiers.

I'll find you new homes with caring neighbors.
I promise to keep in touch, make *snow-bird* visits.
Virginia's clay cannot replace my familiar coquina.
My new home won't be the same without you.

Nature's Passage

I. First day   Virginia creeper high up
captures best seats of vernal season
as wild columbine   sundrops   violets
shimmer to life

Spring paths of   bluebells   wild phlox
dance around dead sticks   abandoned
when woodlands slept   Dogwoods
parade   before peppery weather

II. Summer's lush foliage
explodes in hallelujah chorus
Cardinals   robins   blue jays   bluebirds
sing praises with vibrancy

Mother trees   tulip   maple   oak   hickory
rejoice   in sunshine riot of abundance
Redbud's dramatic music in magenta
sings the season with burgundy pawpaw

III. As daylight diminishes   woods
slump into muted brown Melancholia
choregraphed by kindreds who
reaffirm the life cycle   with comfort of

layers of subdued soil   Landscape
heaves relief   when temperatures
at hasty or restrained pace
drop to cozy repose

Nature's Passage   2 of 2

IV. Like pick-up sticks more trees
    fall betwist   between   in vees of limbs
    not up   not down   in limbo
    held amidst crowning hope and loam

    Green frogs   American toads
    rest in ponds   copperheads in stolen beds Black bears
    in frozen repose
    hibernate   until universal clock rewinds

Full Bloom

Frail seedlings peak
from gritty surface
above shadows
of old growth.

Few thrive amidst
isolating drought
and insects hungry
for naïve blossoms.

But fed ground
fortifies growth,
strengthens roots
beyond neglected past.

Hardihood

I prefer winter . . .
when you feel the bone structure in the landscape
—the loneliness of it—the dead feeling of winter.
Something waits beneath it—the whole story doesn't show.
                                                —Andrew Wyeth

Winter does not tolerate
empty-headed innocence
with inexperienced, untested ideology
   whatsoever.

It's spent too long setting statutes
based on the hard dirt of living
based on practical, sensible
   endeavors.

But, minute flags of color unfurl
in frosted turf, all white with submission
in frozen ponds thick from neglectful
   December.

Incipient flowers flourish with young green leaves
grounded in promise beyond frost-bitten threats,
grounded in fearlessness regardless of
   weather.

Peace

Now I see the secret of making the best person:
it is to grow in the open air
and to eat and sleep with the earth.
—Walt Whitman

Bald eagles stay steadfast sky keepers   no matter
  the seasonal heavens of the Blue Ridge
Wooded breath slows to meditative pace
   under unintentional weight of falling oak leaves
   that lead   parade of accord   at mountains' peaks

Mother trees orchestrate   ants hibernate   beetles
  seek tree eaves and attics   squirrels cache acorns
  humpbacks migrate beyond Atlantic beaches
  black bears hibernate   bass dive deeper
  neighborhood petals and leaves decay in harmony

Some human creatures   hold all Earth as their own
  family   so they protect their brothers and sisters
  from   chemicals   contaminants to pollutants
  that hurt any relative   they make peace
  with inner nature   within human nature

Above the Darkness

Lush forest bed
Alive with skeletons
   fallen leaves
hardened limbs
  broken branches
    scattered
    crushed
    decayed
Mulching tender sprouts
of hope

Road to *Leenan*

They walk along
a shy country road
which meanders
to a forested red bridge
trimmed in tall grasses

and marsh flowers, a favorite
spot to picnic. Stout
rain interrupts respite
and pushes them higher,
one rock-pocked hillside,

the twin of another.
Maamturks and *Sheffry
Hills* hold hands
at *Killary Harbour*,
host to mussels,

wild salmon and politics.
As the harbor becomes
dim spectre, ancient
farm walls dominate descent
to the civilized tarmack

of *Leenan*. Brightly-
colored wooden boats
in the gentle mossback bay
welcome the weary
at journey's end.

Summer in the South of France

fuchsia bougainvillea
a vivid memory of *Villefranche*

so too Mediterranean pastels
washing shoreline cafes with unhurried tourists

ancient specks of paint clinging
stubbornly to the bay's tired dinghies

back alleys lined with window flowers
and breezy webs of laundry lines

congregated in gossip about swarms
of cruise ships intruding like zoo visitors

along the rugged coast and a quick train ride
connects *Villefranche* to *Monaco*

blinks of cliff homes and modest villages
rush by to the steady clatter of track

the *Principality* appears like a postage stamp
neatly placed on a souvenir postcard

the tiny kingdom piled high like Legos
in tight stacks of apartments and offices

Prince Albert's palace towers above
still haunted by the charm of Princess Grace

Three Sisters

Glaciered tendrils
flowing down her back,
old-growth forest
stands proudly more than
10,000 feet high,
shoulders above any
volcanic neighbors.

Whole Soil Web

There is a necessary wisdom in the give-and-take of nature—
its quiet agreements and search for balance.
—Suzanne Simmard

Largest and oldest   Mother Trees   provide for the entire forest
  the wood wide web
  seedlings   saplings   trees   fungi   bugs   creatures

        below   at   above ground

with love for all kindred
   their teats of deep roots and fungi
     quench thirst of   shallow-rooted seedlings
     feed   sugar   carbon   nitrogen   to saplings
     reduce roots in high-traffic areas
     open roads for   flourishing families

without prejudice to species
   share food with immigrant trees
   adapt neighborly help along seasonal shifts
     Douglas Firs   share cups of sugar with Birch
       in spring and fall   Birch   return cups
     of sugar in summer

with memory and intelligence
   use seed DNA and tree rings of diverse species
    to resist   hotter and drier conditions
   despite velocity of global warming   For
   survival of us all   Planet Earth   Mankind
   must cultivate the ways of Mother Trees

        below   at   above ground

2. Fire

We seek the spark
that is already within us.
 —Kamand Kojouri

Acid Brew

*The violence that exists in the human heart
is also manifest in the symptoms of illness that we see in the
Earth, the water, the air and in living things.*
—Pope Francis

of discontent will rise from her scarred belly,
long the brunt of human parasites.
Bile will seep through her earthy pores, nothing
recognizable will remain but crusty derma—

no Redwoods, no Amazon ants, no Sandhill Cranes
no Giant Hare ferns, no Goblin sharks,
no Hula painted frogs who had survived her moods
millions of years.

Expressed in glacier melts and trillion-ton breaks,
in weather fits—5,000 storms, floods, monster winds
in four US months—her seething waters
will accelerate to full boil, then evaporate

like California's drought, the worst
in 1200 years—without watermark regrets—
into deep space as radiant energy,
solar and space drag retaliation

for America's insatiable gluttony each year—
two billion tons of burning fossil fuels,
83 million tons of unrecyclable trash,
and 40 percent pollution of all waters.

Black Hole

cold-hearted air   running   hastily   through the void

refugees resist   approaching visceral fog   last breaths

tumbling   in destiny's wake   vulnerable trees   pace

in frantic   helplessness   lush forest bed   alive with

dead skeletons of   fallen leaves from   hardened limbs

broken branches   scattered   crushed   decayed

deliberate carnage   burying   careful doctrine
partisan scriptures   proclaiming connections
regiments   uncover   signs in the murk
torches of truth diminishing
into oblivion swirling
darkness   abyss
ravenous

Road to *Hana*

The remotest island on the planet
is a familiar place I've never been,

a *déjà vu* homecoming to paradise.
Solid wall of waterfalls on the left,

the Pacific on the right, rainbows—
out my windshield, in my rear

and side mirrors, everywhere,
even stamped on the Aloha state plate.

All the other brown faces with
almond eyes and button noses mark

me part of the tribe's tropical mix,
not the exotic animal I am back home.

Serenity

Legs chewed raw, she sits resigned
not complaining of edges worn brown.
She welcomes light coming her way
past shadows of slugs in the mud.

Ripped patches creep along her veins
until all join forces into one gaping hole.
She never shuns strife. She stands
her ground despite the toll demanded.

We cannot predict our fate
for nature picks the game.
Though daisy's blooms have fallen,
she chooses to live her way.

Bus Stop

A one-legged vet leans at the curb
a caricature of   mutilated plastic
caught in the gutter   no one cares
to clean up

Mother and kids huddle
shaped into incognito cardboard
beaten flat for trash   under the nearby bridge   waiting
just out of sight   just in case

Scattered cigarette fibers   smashed faceless
tell her story   She clutches a stuffed bag
to calm hot panic   rising in her veins
relentless as addiction

Amidst glass   broken
cheap-life sediment
waits for a ride   anywhere but here
where each knows the way   blindfolded

Change of Heart

*Keep a green tree in your heart and
perhaps a singing bird will come.*
— Chinese Proverb

Random worry changes the climate in my brain
Relentless drought scorching my inner landscape
  leaves me seedless for personal growth

    leathered hands   hesitant to hold
    dry eyes   cautious to cry
    parched lips   afraid to sip

Defeated in the gray   half-dead forest of my
  thoughts   slender clouds render
    light tearful rains

    cheer the soil of my soul
    plant seeds of hope
    wash away layers of doubt

Internal sunlight nurtures buds on barren branches
  hints of green on the ground   of my mind
    as hope flourishes

    softened hands   eager to caress
    moistened eyes   shining to smile
    open heart   ready to embrace

As an internal vista cultivates   a spiritual sanctuary
  in my woodlands   all my bodily territories
    bridge in heartfelt peace

Habits of American Habitat

I do many small things just to change my habits . . .
—Greta Thunberg

When I drink my water from a handy plastic bottle
   or a glass at home,
use store retail and grocery bags
   or my own recyclable containers,
buy cheap picnic utensils and supplies
   or use my home provisions,

I add to the more than 5.25 trillion pieces of ocean plastic,
250 million metric tons by 2025   or not.

When I drink my convenient K-Cup coffee
   or brew in a coffeepot,
stop at a fast-food place for take-out
   or bring my brown bag lunch,
buy a frozen, prepackaged meal
   or make a simple dish at home,

I add to the 268 million tons of US garbage
World's #1 in toxic landfills or incinerators or not.

When I grasp a paper towel to swipe a spill
   or cloth rag to clean a spot,
buy eggs in Styrofoam containers
   or get fruit in eco-friendly bags,
cover lunch in plastic wrap
   or store leftovers in old glass jars,

I add to *unrecyclables* in toxic landfills, or worse,
the *25% already polluted* at recyclable sites   or not.

Paradise Lost

On a morning saunter in my yard
a strange sight put me on guard.
Two collared cats stopped my step—
stole buds and promptly left.

A Gerber daisy began to dance,
but closer check showed slugs' advance!
They'd chewed my flowers to nubs—
telltale powder on sickly stubs.

Wilted wildflowers fought new pots,
hated uprooting from parking lots
to—genteel soil, fresh water, part sun.
Broken glass and litter was more fun.

Shade plants stood still,
kept their promise to bloom at will.
But, hostas—ready to flower—were devoured
by sneaky deer in quick order!

I've failed to make nature my friend!
I'm better with plastic, strung end to end.
Fake flowers have no bugs or needs
So I have plenty free time to do as I please.

Nonnative Species

Then, neighborhoods of immigrants wrestled
with American repackaging—a trimming
of fat for better sales in a new world market.

Italians in *guinea*-tees muscled to the prime case
of the butcher shop with popular pepperoni
and prosciutto;

behind storefront homes, Poles peddled
blood soup and *pierogis;* Jews pushed
bagels, pastrami and chicken soup
in corner mama-and-papa delicatessens.

All-American eats, their distinct tastes
are wrapped in US-standard paper.

My Filipino father started
as a dishwasher but became a chef
in first-class restaurants, my dark-skinned uncle
a business owner. My cousin, a dropout,
became department head of a national airline.

Their brown skin bleached
enough to be welcomed in the White world.

Now, 65 million worldwide, 24 per minute,
(more than half children) escape

Nonnative Species

Arab, African, Spanish dead-end borders, adapt
identities like the Darwin survivors
from two world wars.

Foreign-born still sputter English, rely
on community greenhouses to interpret
fast-talking landscapes.

Public schools promise the same gold-starred
futures to foreign-born children as their parents
who take pride in entry-level jobs, like bragging
pigeons pleased to find crumbs on a park bench.

85% work inside five months—

Congolese Charly Ngoma, promoted
to general manager of the Phoenix Chipotle
eighteen months after his US arrival.

In my home town,

Iranians, Parvin and Yadollah Jamalraza, own
a tailor shop; Dominican Tony Pollanco runs
his own catering business, Algerian Mouadh
Benamar researches cancer.

Transplants survive and thrive to flood
a kicking-and-screaming mainstream with
a robust, diverse gene pool.

Clearcutting

Peeling paint on leaning legs
against a corner out of the way,
an empty chair   recalls

her days in green-scented woods.
She'd once been a mighty white oak
intent to live centuries

with neighbors and visitors—
wild turkeys   white-tailed deer   opossums
Blue Jays   Bobwhites   Eastern cottontails.

Loggers leveled and dragged her away—
stripped   chopped   sanded   stained—
pieces of her transformed into

hard   artificial forms.
One was   an occasional chair
sold owner to owner   layered

with paint-masked dings,
an unrecognizable victim
that grew useless   from use   from abuse.

Now outside   repurposed
into a makeshift plant stand
she's resurrected in the sunshine—

visits with feathered friends
revels in the cool rains
remains a mighty white oak.

Extant

With breathless heaviness
leaves surrender
to sudden drop

in pressure before the storm.
Flying in all directions,
startled thoughts

skitter to brittle branches
that might not
hold their weight.

Turbulent blows suddenly
percuss across the trunk,
now vulnerable to whirling

debris. In a downpour,
harsh and heavy,
disappointments rain,

destroying old confidences.
Battered limbs drop, leaving
piles of muddy confusion.

Each storm she
survives the abuse,
rooted in silence.

Lonely George Is Dead

We should bow deeply before the orchid and the snail
... before the monarch butterfly and the magnolia tree.
The feeling of respect for all species will help us
recognize the noblest nature in ourselves.
—Nhat Hanh

From the filthy bilges of merchant ships
came furry invaders that gorged
their bellies with raw natives, overran the islands.

Human gods later brought wolfsnails
to "biocontrol" other island creatures,
as if using one life to kill another were sanctified.

But the wolfsnails disobeyed the human masters
and slayed scores of smaller natives. The gods picked
favorites among the living, like chameleons

As pets, that had huge appetites for little natives.
Loss of forest vegetation by people's pigs and goats drove
native survivors to safety of mountain trees—

a banishment of innocence by entitlement.
The last survivor of a tribe of Hawaiian tree snails,
Achatinella apexfulva—one of the first species

discovered—was kept alive in a lab for 14 years. Lonely George
has now died. Three-fourths of snail species in Hawaii are extinct,
forever dead.

Lonely George Is Dead

Ten remaining species are expected to join George
on the doomsday assembly line this decade. Human deities
may be unconcerned by yet another

foreigner's death until they see tree snails
control fungal abundance and diversity, but survival of the gods
requires turning from their own needs first.

Strip Mall Apocalypse

Hunger for profit chops forests,
fragile from global warming—137
species dying daily.

Profiteers deny devastation
as seasonal shows
where the dead return in the second act.

But, the final performance
will be cancelled. The white-washed
face of urban planning installs

three trees per 10,000 feet,
poster children on
sanitized stages.

We'll be left with playbills,
souvenirs of once live performances—
   wax museums
   movie clips
   stuffed cages.

Subtle songs   vibrant colors   singular scents
will be lost in
   metal
   brick
   glass.

Relentless Winter

Chronic sickness pecks
at the graceful, ripe skin
that binds us.

Pristine sprouts, untried
cures, sustain delicate
deal-making, but, dogged

heat puckers
harsh truths, spoils
fruits before they ripen.

Broken, unsorted
turns of color
settle in weighty drifts.

Vulnerable, the tree
reveals our worried branches
as leaves succumb.

Sun, heavyhearted,
creeps lower each day,
a cloaked warning of cold.

Extended night
cannot be ignored,
despite our extra layers.

Chosen Moments 1 of 2

Amid the universal clatter, the incessant din of business,
the all swallowing vortex of the great money whirlpool-
who has any, even distant, idea of profound repose . . . silence?
—Walt Whitman

Growing up in the inner-city
I dreamed of getting my own home
without tissue paper walls between neighbors
and real grass without glass
on the right side of the tracks

but the house and dreamscape I bought
never stopped my worry over being good enough
A flower child during Vietnam
I believed in our lifetime we would
end war   end famine   end racial inequality

All we had to do was love   but since Nam
there's been twenty-four more major US conflicts
7,900 American dead
Make Love Not War   was killed in action
I was hopeful Kennedy   then King   then Obama

would deliver a free and just land   but I felt buried by White
Supremacist backlash in recent years   tombstoned by a hometown
clash in Charlottesville
These days   I turn off bloodied headlines
sidestep political conversations   no longer expect

Chosen Moments

sloganized peace on earth
     We can do better   urged JFK
     Yes we can   roused Obama
My step back   from mainstream
has brought me moments of peace

lone walks where air kneads step   unhurried strolls
feathered worlds in the forest   to feed
my humility   cleared schedules   to brighten weather forecasts
Small choices
give me peace on this earth

Unseen Seen

It is not freedom from conditions, but . . .
freedom to take a stand toward the conditions.
—Viktor Frankl

Senses sift thoughts into maps
ways to sojourn   Mother Earth

Bundled perceptions lend
contrived sensibility   to choices

amidst fickle realities
like the timeless myth of the 24-hour day

We force delinquent minutes to hide
behind time zones   Clocks seem in step

with the sun—while the Earth's real
elliptical orbit throws out regularity

Racism is justified by   the hyperbole of evolution
Superiority and complexity   mere card tricks

Winning fungi   sharks   mosses
hold same card hand for   millennium

Science popularizes discoveries
in fifteen-minute frames of fame

Sky wears blue   disguises
multi-colored diversity

Aristotle made celebrities of
vision   sound   smell   touch   taste

Unseen Seen   2 of 2

but fifteen more sensory stars should headline—
temperature   time   thirst   pain   pressure

The truth is not absolute
more a shape-shifter of coerced image

Weather-beaten brains do not surrender
learning as old headlines declared

Today's truth   more dead reckoning
of position from distance run

How do we forge direction without
all confirmed colors of   life's prism

free ourselves from prison
of changing circumstance?

Recede into the Noise of Everyday Memory

The unborn child remembered
tender murmurs in the swirled universe
of mother's belly.

Her memory settled in the backbone
of her heart when her mother left.
Empty bites of teen fantasy and adult subtitles

kept her hungry for contentment. Her heart
surrendered to her tough gut to survive
and she lived off man-made products

to lubricate her days with quotas, deadlines
and popularity polls, not visceral longings.
It was when she'd stopped looking

for true sustenance that she heard a rhythm
so faint, she first thought it errant noise.
She didn't hear the rhythm again. She felt it

in the backbone of her heart, in rhythm with hers.
At last together in their elder years, they've forgotten
they were ever apart.

Provocation

*The first step toward success is taken when you refuse to be
a captive of the environment in which you first find yourself.*
—Mark Caine

Between toes
at the foot of twin mountains
then along rawboned trails,
the victimized spasm emboldens,
bulldozes fleshy forests and bloody streams,
demands recompense for careless neglect.

Once a brief downpour could
flush littered streams,
a clearcut of fat trees
revitalize breaths,
or flash fires
destroy negligent leavings.

Now a tsunami of pain rumbles
muscled revolution
against toxic routines.
Environment cleanses
    as sunlit air revives body common,
    apex to underbelly.

Vigor rebounds
    when verdant sinew strengthens,
    canyon floor to summit.
Sustenance amends
    just as fresh growth flourishes,
    fluids to firmament.

Natural order finds its justice.

Up in Smoke

Shaded under sugar maple, yellow birch, magnolia,
the old girl's aged well. Eastern cougar, red wolves
and black bears—her companions all these many years—
with occasional settlers paying respect.

There have been wars and railroad intrusions
to endure—nothing like the stubborn kudzu
of developers and tourists these days. Why ten million
visitors come traipsing

through these parts a year seems like! I worry
about her breathing lately. Her air and streams just don't
seem right since all these money-hungry
people came around her.

Some of her old friends have been chased away for good—the
emerald dragonfly, the Carolina parakeet, the American chestnut.
Some threatened just hide—
woodpeckers, flying squirrels, chubs.

She's been around 300 million years, but folks shouldn't
take her for granted. This great lady,
the Great Smoky Mountains, will end up
in ashes just like us, if we're not careful.

Yoshino Cherry Tree

Many springs ago   a Japanese fairy traveled
to the Blue Ridge Mountains
delicately breathed upon certain trees that
instantly burst into pink blossoms   then cherries

One magical tree lives near me   Decades she gave
cherries to wild critters   She prevailed with curved torso
a testimony to her ripe heart
as she circled   spun   twirled   bowed   to each year

Now forty more years among   small homes
and scattered   sad trees with large dead limbs
she struggles to bear for   human and wild neighbors but
circles   spins   twirls   bows   to each year

Soon she will return to the fairyland of her birth
her torso smooth and upright   her branches uplifted
Vibrant woods will enfold her   as she
circles   spins   twirls   bows   forever

Lunch Encounter

Across from me, a Kurdish refugee, now in D.C., eats pizza. The Cairo woman says she detects his slight American speech while she tries pancakes with a hot dog. Left of me, a Jamaican eats a vegetarian plate as he pitches his show, *Food War,* at small colleges before his visa expires. Two New Yorkers, one Brooklyn and one Bronx, are picking at food, intent on conversation with the Egyptian who's showing cell phone pictures of her brother and his fiancé who is too good for him. Another vegetarian, a Filipino woman from California, and her new Virginia friend join our table, sitting next to an African-American physician-writer from Philadelphia, who piles salt on his buffet choices. Between bites, the three-anecdote segregation where each lives. I am raving about how wonderful the sautéed garlic spinach is, sometimes interjecting my personal experiences as a bi-racial child in the trio's diatribe. Drifting in and out of each other's ordinary conversations, we shrink the globe to plate size.

Making Way

The world rounds into connections
circumstance loops   in closed circuit
a maze begins and ends   in one place

    Decay on the forest floor   births life
    Young shoots writhe   darkness to light

    Dead of night quiets   din of day
    Morning breath flushes into   inky shadows

    Pollution makes   freshness precious
    Less awakens   kinder alternatives

Universality   unveils in opposites
Each coin side   complements the whole
Like yin and yang   halves complete each other

    Budding and well-versed   learn from each other
    Labyrinth of faces   occupies life's circle

    Friend and foe   stand on common ground
    One face of need   the timeless denominator

    Filthy rich and dirt poor   cellmates in mortality
    Money bags don't extend   human border

Yet   righteous insistence on one path prevails
shorter   smarter   easier   cheaper   is touted
like *Cliff Notes* bypass unabridged reading

A Universal of Belonging

All I'm saying is the whole world comes to life:
every kind of cactus, every kind of tree or dead branch,
the sunrise, the sunset, the different kinds of birds.
I find myself in the middle of a universe of belonging.
     —Richard Rohr

Global turbulence disturbs   like an angry mob breaks down
contrived borders among tribes

Individuals are fenced by emergency signs of fear
Peace is elusive   clouded by desparate crises

Resolute warfront defenders   rise along
Virginia frontline

               Red Maple   Black Locust
           Eastern White Pine   Black Oak

Nature is intuitive
with outstretched limbs and roots to comfort

              furred medley   *scaled* diversity
              feathered sorts   *fleshed* tribes

Continent to shore amidst human conflict
nature *rises*   as soft beacons

Along harsh territories
nature *whispers* welcome

               to wellsprings of inner peace
             without prejudice   to all clans

3. Air

We all inhabit the planet.
We all breathe the same air.
—John F. Kennedy

Mountainous Hush

Emaciated wisps of clouds sway
like frayed ropes stretching from
verdant forest floor to idle sky.

Clean green enlivens the Virginia
Creeper's mood as it curls fir
branches, tickles the oak's mossy

beard. Despite the heckles of
feathered whistlers and occasional
groans of streams delayed by rocks,

the patient pillars of granite and
unfazed, ancient red clay protect
the Blue Ridge's voluminous quiet.

A Seed for a Seed

Blue Jays   war lords of sky   terrorize all who fly
for more   more land   more food   more air
They are born to take   not negotiate

When distracted by a clutch of young
the neighbors are grateful for the ceasefire
Well-fed bystander   Gray Catbird

does nothing but eye two Chickadees   bullied
by a male Cardinal   hell-bent intent on shoving
them off the feeder for its own fledgling

That there is enough   does not matter
What matters is
his turf   his father's   and his father's

Black-headed Chickadees are   not welcome
The male leaves the Purple Finch alone
on another foothold   her reddish head

remotely   Cardinal red   helps the female
avoid profiling   camouflaged in the trees' recess
Field Sparrows subsist best

by waiting   for crumbs forgotten
So too   the Tufted Titmouse scouts
from leafy cloak   its gray-black markings

A Seed for a Seed   2 of 2

easily spotted by enemy bomber
Half the size of most rivals   the Titmouse
allies with Chickadees and Nuthatches

Robins retain territory   by split-second shifts
consume anything available
bug in midair   poison ivy and grubs   fruits and fish

align with Cedar Waxwings for spoils
bunk in the Common Grackle's old nest
The Mourning Dove   solitary pacifist

lingers on the ground   avoids skirmishes
eats abreast foreigners
assured there's sufficient seed for all

Do You Hear the Birds?

*"Do you hear the birds?" . . . it has become a way
of reminding ourselves that Nature's
healing presence is always just outside.*
—Donnalee B.

My old bones   worried and wearied from
deep-rooted pangs   commiserate with each other
yet compete for attention like game contestants

Injuries charted on my skeletal graph are used
as handy reference   for cranky arguments
among players to win   bragging rights

for my worst suffering   Clamor from aging
joints and shaggy muscles   clenches my feelings
clouds my thoughts

shoves me into murky isolation
Hushed shadows   slither in my cranial cave
deepen despair   deaden hope   for peace of mind

Suddenly a faint note distracts my cacophony
seduces my agitated gray matter   My eyes
squint toward backyard trees   along the quiet creek

Minute movement amidst branches   awakens me
to layered song   away   from my head chatter
a crimson cardinal call

cheer cheer cheer   purdy purdy purdy
then a bluejay winging away   *jeer jeer jeer*
mingled with house wrens   *zureee zureee zureee*

Do You Hear the Birds?

Spellbound by the rhapsody   I sit by the open
window breathing in the melodic drifts
no longer white noise to my angst but   calming

sounds that cleanse my spirit   My face softens
sways to nature's rhythm   I join the chorus with
my own effortless hums   Their song becomes mine

Gilded Silver Face

Yellow Garden Spider

The entire universe is one ecosystem,
similar to a spider web—if one part is touched,
the entire net shimmers.
— Matthew Flickstein

I. Stretched to the shadow line of horizon
   she sways in breathy waves
   snug in surroundings

   Her long legs tucked in tall grasses
   shadowed from sight and sun
   like shrouded thought

   Sunny fields gleam nearby   smile
   a warm welcome for visitors to enter
   her new circular home   adorned in

   silks and layered zigzag patterns
   Glamorous elegance center stage
   She entertains   a carnivorous banquet

   gnats   mosquitoes   flies   aphids
   sides of butterflies and beetles
   on fine samite platters

   Even when geckos and green anoles
   come to call   her home embraces all
   like a wide net

Gilded Silver Face

Yellow Garden Spider

II. A male suitor recently built nearby
    strums away for the spotlight
    hopes for a spark   hangs a distance

    from a drop line in case
    his subtle quivers cause her disgust
    She falls for his pursuits

    intimacy   immediate but brief
    like steamy gossip whispered in an ear
    He weakens in her arms   but soon dies

    Her legs wrap their unborn
    in glossy sheets   until their spring birth
    Tiny as dust   gathered in a silk blanket

    young scatter   everywhere
    some near   some far   wherever
    the breeze carries them

    Mother stays in her zigzag dome
    bundled until   her sunny fields return

Drakes

dodge watchful eye of
rainbow trout in the shadows,

like helicopters
rise and dip,

drop eggs
along water's skin.

Newborns sprout wings,
quickly soar from wet nest,

continue one-day cycle of
Mayflies.

Nest Building

one broken branch
held up by others

every bit as twisted
dried grass in gaps

red mud for mortar
lined in spotted leaves

each important
for the whole

Fogbound

Luminescent white droplets roll lazily,
create a surreal glow that envelops us.
At the gate of thick morning fog, pearl air
caresses creamy waters, beckons us closer.

Once inside, a perfect white-on-white rainbow
permeates the haze like the sun's flashlight.
Graceful dolphins rise at the bow, mimic
the ivory archway.

Unconcerned pelicans float in and out of fog,
like lifeless driftwood rising and falling
then rest on a remote beach. Seagulls rise
from the mist, haunt the shifting edge of fog.

Swallowed by Deadman's Channel off Cedar Key,
we are hostages in a fifth dimension—
ghost markers and muddled voices
of failed boat motors and crashing waves.

Only gentle wind and sea keep us moving,
searching for escape. Non sequitur thoughts zigzag,
ways to freedom, ways to die.
No fresh water. No food left. Useless paper map.

Just as we'd eased into the white trap, we spot
the smallest patch of blue, then a scant
shadow of land until the Channel mercifully
brings us back to full-colored space and time.

Pileated Pearls

Amidst dusty hush
of pine needle floor

stands old growth firs
riddled with holes

like gems strung
in twisted ropes.

Silence breached,
the woodpecker

is revealed by
each precision drill.

Surviving the Unsurvivable

A bugle call in 2007 in the dead of night
from diseases   pesticides   fewer florals
stifled bee hives   worldwide

Colony Collapse Disorder forced
global attention to   honeybees   pandemic
pacesetters that are 80% of all pollinators

Worker bees and queens are   leaving nests
larvae are dying   Global warming whirls
honeybees' life-giving syrup

down a perverted drain   Accepted since ancient
Egypt   immortal honey houses
thousands of enzyme armies to—

eliminate toxins   host adaptable antibiotics
avoid memory or mood ditches   keep humans
alive for a day   on one fuel-efficient spoonful

Except honeybees especially wild honeybees
face a forever and ever   global expiration
if left to us   who watch   who do nothing

Nature's Eye

Pine needles cushion my sunny repose
on a shy boulder of Old Rag Granite peaking
through lichen and moss.

Thousands of Blue Ridge trees—buried knee deep
in brittle curls of leaves—muffle distant roars of big
water accustomed to rule.

Innocent air brushes my face like the first flickers of
an emerging butterfly—soft strokes against my
eyelashes, tender whispers through my curls.

Wildlife rests in shadows but for infrequent flying
specters that suggest legions of life share this
moment with me in the woodlands.

The Moon

pulls the tides close
to her bosom, caresses
shore each night in waves

of delight as the stars
brighten in the glow
of cosmic lovemaking
until dawn interrupts

How she cherishes
the embrace
every evening
of sea and sky

Universal Language

Inspired by Oliver Sacks, Musicophilia

Two million years of musical
rhythm compose visceral
understanding underneath

man's survival stance,
a spontaneous response like turtle
hatchlings drawn to sea.

Even before language, like
a human flesh denominator
melodic tempos captured all cultures.

In the womb, the unborn dance
to notes and beats—inherent
as honeybees dancing towards

a food source. Harmonics tie
all groups. People move
in collective excitement, all cued

by rhythms, internalized as one
jukebox. Concerts, marches, dirges
choreograph brain waves

   like birds in formation,
   like fish in schools,
   like monarchs in migration.

Universal Language

Tune transcends disease. People
with aphasia sing, with Tourette's
drum, with retardation dance,

with dementia remember. Music
fights back. Man's humanity survives
without symbol or instruction.

Tropical Toll

Florida deer froze in wide-eyed terror,
waited for the grave advance
of the head-on hurricane
the Caribbean in its wreckage.

But the six-hundred-mile giant
rolled past   rampaged
the eastern coastline,
cast a wake of dark

torrid seas and tornadoes—
a souvenir of its howling savagery.
The tiny-hoofed beasts released
breath before another headlight fury.

One

*Life shrinks or expands
in proportion to one's courage.*
　　　　　—Anais Nin

ear hears another voice. One
hand touches a stranger's. One
foot follows more. One
common trauma bubbles into one
boiling effort, the masses in one
scalded demise by the silvered spoons, every one.

One
emboldens one
soft-spoken who encourages one
considered broken to come. One
elder listens to one
young who brings one
outed into the rung. One
persuades her almond-eyed friend afar. That one
wins over one
slightly inky sister, who hooks one
mixed-up stranger until one
earthen vessel lifts us all as one.

4. Water

*You are not a drop
in the ocean.
You are the entire ocean
in a drop.*
—Rumi

Confluence

Early thawed waters
wander in muddy confusion.
Disappointed bald cypress branches

deepen the sludge.
Tulip poplar buds fall
to the thin-skinned surface

as a dispirited stream swirls
slowly nowhere.
Entanglements trapped in eddies

despair along ragged banks.
Maple colors begin
to calm the creek's drift.

Settled waters open the way
to merge with another
in life's winter solstice.

Holy Place

Cabo de Sao Vincente, Portugal

Vertical cliffs rise 75 feet from the Atlantic,
a landmark for Mediterranean ships and sacred

ravens who kept vigil for a fourth-century
Christian martyr. Abundant nests on the craggy

walls bring—rare Bonelli's eagles, peregrine
falcons and rock thrushes—their wings stirring

a hurricane of feathers in the mist. Already
sacred in Neolithic times—the Greeks called

it the Land of the Serpents, the Romans, Holy
Promontory. Marking the edge of their world,

they held it a magical place where the sun sank
hissing into the ocean

Passing lobster vessels continue homage
to the only God of earth and sea.

Ivy Creek

Bleached fir limbs scatter   in twisted piles along
my path   half covered by leafy centuries
their khaki secrets whispered   season to season
among the creatures that crawl beneath

Annual death toll is disguised by—
stately elm   wide-armed oak   prolific tulip poplar
The ground is peppered   with ostrich and wood fern
Greenery itself is a soothing saunter

Amidst gentle air   ever-so-distant—
   banter of a woodpecker's *rat-a-tat-tat*
   persistent tree-to-tree *whistle* of a red-hot cardinal
mix with the steady pulse of   a mountain stream

Rejuvenated by nature's cacophony   I linger
in the thick of green   hope to absorb
some element of wisdom in its visceral order
follow   my own thumbprint of life

Loxahatchee

Above Trapper Nelson's thick overhang
the sun blazes white causing
mist to rise from logs   like primeval specters
the river to shimmer like tinsel on sweaty trees

Centuries-old cypress pose
as wild bronze beauties
black-muck hair   adorned with
giant ferns   white lilies   spiders' glistening lace

Beneath her surface beauty runs
impetuous dead ends   furtive gator holes
rushing dams   fallen wooden giants
that pop out like carnival rides   adding to her allure

The Loxahatchee tidal river sanctuary
is a 64-acre private chapel for
pileated red-headed woodpeckers   elusive panther
manatee   fierce water moccasins

Paddlers usually spot
blue heron   egret   ibis
wood storks   peregrine   falcons
rarely surface

The Northwest Fork of the Loxahatchee
was to be restored to its pristine state long ago
but even one step toward environmental healing
still offers hope.

Palma de Mallorca

Beseiged by summer Europeans
for its pearls and leather, this
cosmopolitan port off Spain discourages

exploring—her mountainous inner
beauty blocked by breathtaking drops
and hairpin turns, much like Rapunzel's

fortified tower. Cutting rocky terrain,
tourist trains, do manage rare glimpses
of old olive gardens, cliff estates,

countless villages hidden from shore.
For centuries well-protected from pirates,
popular *Valdemossa,* honors its good

fortune to local St. Catherine by hanging
her tiled image in every home. Terrace
farming and uniform sandy pink structures

speak softly of former monastic traditions.
This reclusive quietude drew Chopin and
lover Sand, later poet Ruben Dario,

writer Jorge Luis Borges, and composer
Josef Horowitz. The search for undisturbed
beauty and creative meditation transform

this Mediterranean isle into a mecca for
treasure hunters—peg-legged, paint-stained,
Hawaiian-shirted, or leather-jacketed.

Matolius River

Gin-clear water crashes
a dignified gathering of Western Larch

Ponderosa and Lodge Pole Pines
in the Deschutes National Forest.

Disorderly lava rock gathers as dramatic
backdrop to—stunning purple lupine

red columbine and Yellow Arrowhead Balsamroot
without a glance from the boisterous river.

The wild and sedately curious
converge to enjoy the river party.

Mosquito Coast

Like surreal strobe lights capturing half-truths,
the road to the Conch Republic hooks both
plastic-flamingo and native grace.
Tourist headlights create silhouettes

of dwarf deer, forever there at dusk grazing
highway one. Another true native, mangroves—
the Atlantic-Gulf nursemaids—quietly tend to—
snapper, crab, tube coral, turtle grasses.

The coastline face lift of jet-ski and moped youth
is tempered by the backwaters
of these glacier-born mangroves
that slow-flow tidal wisdom

to sustain yet revitalize life in the Keys.
More than 100 million domestic
and 10 million foreign visitors
speed or cruise to this tropical paradise.

Orcas

circle   the boat

push   a log

string kelp   with fins

snort laughter   through blowholes

spyhop   a better look

share   this rare sunny day

   in the San Juans

Penny the Shrimp

for our children

—*after* Penaeus Setiferus, *White Shrimp*

White shrimp spawning in Gulf water swells
A million purple eggs straight to the bottom fell.
Itsy bitsy larvae all hatched in half a day.
One rare shrimp arose, showed them the way.

Her name was Penny but mighty for her size.
So strong, she survived many dangers in disguise.
Immortal styrofoam and plastics in the sea,
big fish and loggerheads wouldn't let her be.

She learned tough lessons, man was not a friend.
Farmers and builders, tourists all pretend
Mother Earth's bounty would always be at hand,
nothing need be done, no actions ever banned.

Penny drew the young, from fish to octopi,
called land critters and all birds that fly,
led them to deep water or a hidden place.
Their absence brought panic, folk talked face to face.

They all worked together to respect Mother Earth.
Penny showed the loss, if the planet wasn't first.
Sky is the limit when you stand up for what's true.
Big and small matter, keeping Earth green and blue.

Road from *Lisboa*

Without deference to tourists,
sobreiro cortiça stripped half-naked—
oak bark to red skin—line parched roads,
Lisboa to the Algarve.

So too, indifferent Moors haunt hillside
architecture gently rolling towards the sea,
its beaches—untouchable beauties—
too wild and dangerous to get close.

But, Portuguese fishermen are quick
to share their catch, *espardarte*—
fresh swordfish—with strangers
under the southern crepuscular light.

St. Joe Shore

Atop eighty-foot powder drifts down Cape San Blas
majestic white dunes stretch effortlessly
like a lazy feline in repose   All are adorned with

berries on spiky fir clusters like golden fish eggs
burnt orange grasses that anchor delicate
green fungi in a Monet dream

Gnarled half-buried trunks host elusive deer
as hinted by faint hoof prints   Gulf beaches hoard
clues of its shy inhabitants—

horseshoe crab carcasses pickpocketed by birds
iridescent shell bits decorating the feet of dunes
pebbled treasures tumbling into nameless potpourri

At dusk fog launders land and sea
in an alabaster wash   sheltering living treasures
of this Gulf peninsula

Rainy Days

Dark clouds of late summer
line up like school children
waiting turns to play
afternoon hide-and-seek
with the Florida sun.

Outmaneuvered
by heavy September scape,
red morning skies
are no match for the crowds of rain
gathering for the games.

Day after day, the rains score,
their team colors—blue and gray—
victoriously splashed everywhere
while the sun hopelessly
hides in utter defeat.

Riverview Park Trail

With sleight of hand   summer shifts to hot exhales
and occasional cool breaths across sunburnt
sycamore   red maple   poplar leaves
all gnarled in fisty knots

on the parched Rivanna River trail
Once tallest   most prolific   most prized tree
among Monacan Indians   tulip poplar leaves
tumble to shore   like all others when time to die

One dappled leaf dallies   then flickers off
to goldenrod flowers   a butterfly   mistaken
for a dead leaf   not yet ready
to leave this life

Nearby atop mid-river rocks   geese cavort
over breakfast   clatter to tell   the latest gossip
from a different gang   The feathered coffee klatch
is a welcome respite for resident Canadian geese

Such messy guests   are targeted in Virginia
as legal kills   A morning sidekick
Who doesn't mind the mayhem
is a great blue heron   One leg in practiced bend

she stands still   Her eyes pierce water's surface
as she waits for a kill   in her cross hairs
A patient but insatiable hunter
she glides to her next meal

Fisheating Creek

Dew's coolness heightens anticipation
as the canoe slips into chocolate silk water
like a slow, meandering water snake coiling
through cypress, its tongue taking in all
the primordial sensations.

The ash and mahogany canoe encounters hordes
of buzzards crouched high up on barren limbs
like body bags. Great Blue Herons and Pink-Billed
Ibis fly just ahead—instinct driving them from this
floating intruder.

The lone hawk's warning cry excites
Gray-Speckled Limpkins and Black-and-White
winged Wood Storks who stumble into lift-off,
their shadows painted beneath magnificent wing
spans. Florida wildlife huddles among

lichen-spotted conifers, heavy with air plants and
majestic live oaks, their muscular arms sweating
in afternoon's humid haze. Soaking in white-hot sun,
a lone alligator smiles then slips into cooler waters
near the boat. Everywhere at water's edge are—

bustling cities of butterflies, ominous planets
of hornets, well-fed spiders from overhanging
branches. Near journey's end, the craft is cemented
in place by strong, blustery winds then coughed up
unharmed, eager for another adventure.

St. Patrick's Well

The Twelve Bens, Ireland

Stone Celtic crosses   stand vigil around
St. Patrick's Well   a holy place
atop a vista revealing the Atlantic
in a brief parting of teasing clouds

A statue of young St. Patrick calls pilgrims
to climb towards spiritual solace atop
The Twelve Bens   broad-shouldered mountain tops
holding back dark Irish skies

Rocky Maamturks giants   each with distinct face   lead to
Kylemore Pass   through
thick forest patches and primitive stone fences
ignored by plentiful sheep

past abandoned farmhouses and bountiful streams
rushing from every angle to the sea
Folks from around the world   gather to hear God
speak to them   in the Gaelic of Emerald panoramas

Ten Thousand Islands

skirt the southern Everglades, like a slip's
fine lace edging a shapely beauty. We follow
Alligator Alley, shadowed by the River of Grass—
immortalized by Marjory Stoneman Douglas.

Its steadfast stillness is interrupted by bingo
and Chief Billy's pit stops, like trees cleared
for tourist billboards. Solitary Kingfishers dot
every third pole—sitting motionless afternoons

to strike—as if posed for postcards. Mangroves
become nurseries in step with tidal cadence—
high tide casting leafy chandeliers alit with waterfowl,
low tide exposing mangrove legs,

heavy with oysters and crab traps. Wading birds
delight in a feeding frenzy for delicacies
in low tide's wincing black muck, similar to a
holiday mob overturning a sales rack.

We stay the night in a huddle of mobile homes,
made more alluring by nearby Larry's Famous
Everglades Chikee Bar, nothing but a thatched
haven for cold brews and afternoon fish tales.

More memorable than the Seminole Indian hut was
the Guinness Book mosquitoes that bullied us all night.
At dawn, we snaked mangrove islands and oyster bars
by the Barron and Blackwater rivers.

Ten Thousand Islands

Dark rivers hid—Snook, Red Fish, Speckled Trout.
The Osprey and Devil Birds out-fished us for we
caught only juvenile Yellow Tail Snapper and
an albino Eel. We headed home empty-handed

but filled with ten thousand gifts—the best fried
oysters, skilled bug brigades, the final blood-red
sunset driving home, singing Sgt. Pepper's
Lonely Hearts Club Band on the way.

Sultry Suwanee

The paddle explores big oaks
fringed in long
hair-fine roots that shimmy
in exotic dance

like dark-skinned beauties
in veiled shade
Water in the cypress corridor
is adorned

with sequined iridescent dragonflies
flittering for insect bits
mostly mosquitoes   often moths
butterflies   bees   even other dragonflies

Mulatto sediment
whirlpools with clear springs
swirls murky patterns   along river edge
at shrouded dens   produces diverse banks

one side   soft rolls   another   angular squares
Deeper inland   the wildlife refuge restores
long-leaf pine and wire grass   boosts
giant bat caves   as safe homes

Sultry Suwanee 2 of 2

pollinator gardens   promotes return
of monarchs and swallowtails
Recovery heartens
the flow of river vigor

Native otter   eagle
endangered salt marsh vole   return
whitetail deer again   gaze through grass
All quicken   community breath

Water Percolates Existence

To me the sea is a continual miracle;
The fishes that swim—the rocks—the motion of the waves—
the ships, with men in them, what stranger miracles are there?
—Walt Whitman

Streams *flow* in random turns
*force r*esourcefulness among unrelated tribes—
   Tendrils of Maidenhair   *welcome* dew's kiss.
   Maples   *surrender* to seasonal rains

   seed to sleep to seed   repeat.
   Douglas firs   *never undress.*
   Garden snails   *persist* for millennia
   in fine mucous coats.

From the source   tributaries   *encircle—*
fallen Cypress   overrun trails   blistered outcrops.
Currents *stay* the way   carved
along hard-working banks. Others *integrate* clear

then muddy lagoons   aligned to lunar rhythms.
Each—its own body of water—*sculpts*
uncommon landscapes
a unique tongue prints' bumps and ridges.

Amidst distinct expression   thirst
gathers them into   one ocean   as interlaced seas
life and death   war and peace   same sea of
sense and nonsense   synchronized to the tides.

About the Author

Patsy Asuncion's collections, *Cut on the Bias* (Laughing Fire Press, 2015) and *Lineage of Weeds* (National Media Services Inc. 2023), and her feature in the anthology *The Best 64 Poets of 2019*, depict her world slant as a biracial, first-generation immigrant. She wants to thank her friends and colleagues for their generous support, encouragement, and inspiration.

Patsy promotes diversity in her written and community work. Her publication credits include *The New York Times, About Place Journal, Cutthroat, Artemis, Prevention, Indiana University, Fredericksburg Literary, New Verse News, Vox Poetica,* and 20+ anthologies. She's given presentations at Indiana Writers, Centennial VA Writers, State Poetry Societies, Miami Actor's Theater, DC Split This Rock, and Oklahoma's Woody Guthrie Festival. Her other activities include her open mic (25,200+ YouTube views); community programs with Nasty Women Poets and Social Justice Poets; and involvement in arts boards, adult poetry judging, and collaborative artists-in-residency judging.

Her website is:
patasuncion.wix.com/patsy-asuncion

www.ingramcontent.com/pod-product-compliance
Lightning Source LLC
Chambersburg PA
CBHW072201160426
43197CB00012B/2481